CW01262576

A Management Committee Deliberating

Ackoff's F/laws

The Cake

RUSSELL L. ACKOFF

with Herbert J. Addison

Published in this first edition in 2011 by:

Triarchy Press
Station Offices
Axminster EX13 5PF
United Kingdom
+44 (0)1297 631456

Copyright © Triarchy Press Limited

The right of Russell Ackoff and Herbert Addison to be identified as the authors of this book has been asserted by them in accordance with the Copyright, Designs and Patents Act, 1988.

All rights reserved.

No part of this publication may be reproduced, stored in a retrieval system or transmitted in any form or by any means including photocopying, electronic, mechanical, recording or otherwise, without the prior written permission of the publisher.

A catalogue record for this book is available from the British Library.

ISBN: 978-1-908009-53-1
Drawings by Russell Ackoff

info@triarchypress.com
www.triarchypress.com
www.f-laws.com

Introduction

Over time I have become aware of some very important truths about the practice of management. These truths, which I call the "F/laws of Management," contradict assumptions that are commonly held by managers.

I decided to set down these f/laws because I fear that they will not otherwise be transmitted to the next generation of managers. And I would like future generations of managers to know what of importance I have learned through hard experience.

If readers find any errors either of commission or omission it is my hope that they will let us know. We want to keep this list complete, current, and correct.

These simple management truths are much more important than the fundamental, but complex, truths revealed by scientists, economists, politicians, or philosophers. The truths these wise thinkers reveal are at most frosting on the cake. The truths presented here are the cake.

Russell Ackoff

The Boss from below

Editor's note

In publishing this definitive collection of Russ Ackoff's f/laws, we have reverted to his typescript and used his original form of words and spelling wherever possible (including the use of the term f/law spelt thus).

So that each f/law can stand alone, we have used the full, original text of each one, even if it sometimes overlaps with ideas in another f/law. We have also retained from the two printed collections the numbering of the f/laws except in one place. The f/law formerly known as Number 73 has been deleted because it was duplicated elsewhere. Number 123 has been moved up to 73 to take its place.

A very few of the f/laws (mainly relating to secretaries and telephones) have been somewhat overtaken by change and technology. We've chosen to keep them as they remain, nonetheless, true.

The text of the Introduction on the previous page was, unaccountably, not originally published and we can only hope that Ackoff would have approved of the book's title, which is derived from that Introduction.

To honour Ackoff's desire to keep the list of f/laws up to date, we are again collecting new f/laws contributed by readers. For more information, and to submit your own suggestions, please visit www.f-laws.com or contact me.

Michelle Smith
michelle@triarchypress.com

The Ingredients

Rank has its privileges

Ackoff's F/laws: The Ingredients

1. You can't teach an old dog or executive new tricks, or even that there *are* any new tricks.

2. Knowledge is of two types, explicit and implicit, and knowing this is implicit.

3. You rarely improve an organization as a whole by improving the performance of one or more of its parts.

4. There is no point in asking consumers – who do not know what they want – to say what they want.

5. All managers believe they can do their boss's job better than their boss can, but they forget that their subordinates share the same belief about themselves.

6. For managers the only conditions under which experience is the best teacher are ones in which no change takes place.

7. The level of conformity in an organization is in inverse proportion to its creative ability.

8. The best reason for recording what one thinks is to discover what one thinks and to organize it in transmittable form.

9. No corporation should retain a business unit that is worth more outside the corporation than within it.

10. The amount of irrationality that executives attribute to others is directly proportional to their own.

11. The future is better dealt with using assumptions than forecasts.

12. An organization's planning horizon is the same as its CEO's retirement horizon.

13. The lower the rank of managers, the more they know about fewer things. The higher the rank of managers, the less they know about many things.

14. The importance of executives is directly proportional to the size of their waiting rooms and the number of intervening secretaries.

15. When managers say something is obvious, it does not mean that it is unquestionably right, but rather that they are unwilling to have it questioned.

16. The less sure managers are of their opinions, the more vigorously they defend them.

17. The more lawyers an organization employs, the less innovation it tolerates.

18. Good teachers produce skeptics who seek questions; management gurus produce only disciples, who seek answers.

19. The only thing more difficult than starting something new in an organization is stopping something old.

20. Acceptance of a recommended solution to a problem depends more on the manager's trust of its source than on the content of the recommendation or the competence of its source.

21. The less managers understand their business, the more variables they require to explain it.

Ackoff's F/laws: The Ingredients

22. The higher the rank of managers, the less is the distance between their offices and their restrooms.

23. Business schools are as difficult to change as cemeteries, and for the same reasons.

24. Curiosity is the "open sesame" to learning, even for managers.

25. The legibility of a male manager's handwriting is in inverse proportion to his seniority.

26. Executives must be prevented from receiving any information about frauds or immoral acts committed by their subordinates.

27. There is nothing that a manager wants done that educated subordinates cannot undo.

28. The more corporate executives believe in a free (unregulated) external market, the more they believe in a regulated internal market.

29. The amount of time a committee wastes is directly proportional to its size.

30. It is generally easier to evaluate an organization from the outside-in than from the inside-out.

31. Development is less about how much an organization has than how much it can do with whatever it has.

32. Smart subordinates can make their managers look bad no matter how good they are, and make their managers look good no matter how bad they are.

33. In an organization that disapproves of mistakes, but identifies only errors of commission, the best strategy for anyone who seeks job security is to do nothing.

34. The best organizational designers are ones who know how to beat any organization designed by others.

35. The offense taken by an organization from negative press is directly proportional to its truthfulness.

36. The less important an issue is, the more time managers spend discussing it.

37. The time spent waiting to get into an executive's office is directly proportional to the difference in rank between the executive and the one waiting to get in.

38. Administration, management and leadership are not the same thing.

39. In acquisitions the value added to the acquired company is much more important than the value added to the acquiring company.

40. Business schools are high security prisons of the mind.

41. No matter how large and successful an organization is, if it fails to adapt to change, then, like a dinosaur, it will become extinct.

42. The size of a CEO's bonus is directly proportional to how much more the company would have lost had it not been for him or her.

43. The less managers expect of their subordinates, the less they get.

44. The amount of money spent to broadcast a television or radio commercial is inversely related to its truthfulness and relevance.

45. The more managers focus on how hard their subordinates work, to the exclusion of how much they play, learn and are inspired on the job, the less productive their work is likely to be.

46. A bureaucrat is one who has the power to say "no" but none to say "yes."

47. Teleconferencing is an electronic way of wasting more time than is saved in travel.

48. The more important the problem that a manager asks consultants for help on, the less useful and more costly their solutions are likely to be.

49. The distance between managers' offices is directly proportional to the difference between the ranks of their occupants.

50. The *sine qua non* of leadership is talent, and talent cannot be taught.

51. Managers who don't know how to measure what they want settle for wanting what they can measure.

52. A great big happy family requires more loyalty than competence, but a great big happy business requires more competence than loyalty.

53. If an organization must grow, it is better for it to grow horizontally than vertically.

54. Corporate development and corporate growth are not the same thing and neither requires the other.

55. The uniqueness of an organization lies more in what it hides than what it exposes.

56. The telephone, which once facilitated communication, now increasingly obstructs it.

57. Managers cannot learn from doing things right, only from doing them wrong.

58. The principal objective of corporate executives is to provide themselves with the standard of living and quality of work life to which they aspire.

59. The principal obstruction to an organization getting to where its managers most want it to be lies in the minds of its managers.

60. A corporation's external boundaries are generally much more penetrable than its internal ones.

61. It is very difficult for those inside a box to think outside of it.

62. The level of organizational development is directly proportional to the size of the gap between where the organization is and where it wants to be.

63. Most stated, corporate objectives are platitudes – they say nothing, but hide this fact behind words.

64. Most corporations and business schools are less than the sum of their parts.

65. Managers who try to make themselves look good by making others look bad, generally look worse than those they try to make look bad.

66. The morality that many managers espouse in public is inversely proportional to the morality they practice in private.

Ackoff's F/laws: The Ingredients

67. The higher their rank, the less managers perceive a need for continuing education, but the greater their need for it.

68. The number of references and citations in a book is inversely proportional to the amount of thinking the author has done.

69. No computer is smarter than those who program it. Those who program computers are seldom smarter than those who try to use their output.

70. Managers cannot talk and listen at the same time; in fact, most managers find it very difficult to listen even when they are not talking.

71. Overheads, slides and PowerPoint projectors are not visual aids to managers. They transform managers into auditory aids to the visuals.

72. Conversations in a lavatory are more productive than those in the boardroom.

73. In advertising, all competing products or services have a common property: each is better than all the others.

Ackoff's F/laws: The Ingredients

74. The press is the sword of Damocles that hangs over the head of every organization.

75. The more managers try to get rid of what they don't want, the less likely they are to get what they do want.

76. Focusing on an organization's "core competency" diverts attention from its core competencies.

77. The greater the fee paid to corporate directors, the less their contributions are likely to be.

78. A manager's fear of computers is directly proportional to the square of his/her age.

79. Most managers know less about managing people than the conductor of an orchestra does.

80. Complex problems do not have simple solutions, only simple minded managers and their consultants think they do.

81. When nothing can make things worse, anything can make them better.

82. To do more of what is not working currently, is to do more of what will not work in the future.

83. Those who successfully managed a company to maturity are unlikely to be able to manage it back to youth.

84. Maldistribution of the work-life balance reduces morale and results in poor quality products and services.

85. Greed at the top is the fuel used to increase the maldistribution of wealth within and between corporations, and within and between societies.

86. Viewing the same thing differently is not a defect: it is an advantage.

87. It is better to dissolve a problem than solve it.

88. Giving managers the information needed to (dis)solve a problem does not necessarily improve their performance.

89. The best way to find out how to get from here to there is to find out how to get from there to here.

Ackoff's F/laws: The Ingredients

90. The best place to begin an intellectual journey is at its end.

91. Necessity may be the mother of invention, but invention is the father of desire.

92. Managers should never accept the output of a technologically-based support system unless they understand exactly what the system does and why.

93. The amount of profit that can be got from the sale of a product or service is inversely proportional to the need for it.

94. Meetings that share ignorance cannot produce knowledge.

95. Employees, and even managers, are not expected to be smarter than their bosses.

96. Continuous improvement is the longest distance between two points: where an organization is and where it wants to be.

97. Benchmarking is a not-very-subtle form of imitation. It condemns organizations to following not leading.

98. Consensus is practical, not necessarily principled, agreement.

99. In a classroom, the teacher learns most.

100. There is never a better place to initiate a change than where the one who asks where the best place is, is.

101. Risk aversion is a core competency of most managers.

102. The more managers believe that society should be operated democratically, the less they believe that corporations should be.

103. The one thing that every individual and organization must want is the ability to obtain whatever they want.

104. There is no such thing as risk-free agreement.

105. CEOs should never select their successors.

106. To managers, an ounce of information is worth a pound of data.

107. To managers, an ounce of knowledge is worth a pound of information.

108. To managers, an ounce of understanding is worth a pound of knowledge.

109. To managers an ounce of wisdom is worth a pound of understanding.

110. Giving managers the information they want may not improve their performance.

111. Rightsizing consists of wronging a right.

112. Improving communication between the parts of an organization may destroy it.

113. The stability of a family business and of the family that owns it are inversely proportional to the number of family members employed in the business.

114. Communication is never good in itself.

115. The prominence of a business author is proportional to the number of times he or she has published the same article or book.

116. Organizations fail more often because of what they have not done than because of what they have done.

117. The quality of a business school is inversely proportional to the amount of teaching its faculty does and is directly proportional to the amount of on-the-job learning in which the faculty and students engage.

118. Successful management consultants are ones who support managers' unsupportable beliefs.

119. Problems are not objects of experience, but mental constructs extracted from it by analysis.

120. It is better to control the future imperfectly than to forecast it perfectly.

121. Competition is conflict embedded in cooperation.

122. How far an organization can evade government regulations is proportional to the amount it contributed to the election of successful candidates.

The Cake

Mgr. conducting a cacophony

1. You can't teach an old dog or executive new tricks, or even that there *are* any new tricks.

Most senior executives are relatively near retirement. The less there is of one's future, the smaller is the number of ideas that are seen as new. Eventually, as an executive's professional future approaches zero, there appears to be nothing new under the sun and, therefore, nothing new worth trying. In other words: the future increasingly comes to be perceived as a repetition of the past.

This results in the "We tried it and it didn't work" syndrome. Executives and managers are reluctant to make changes whose effects will not be realized until after their retirement because such changes will have no effect on their reputations and on the bonuses they receive on departure.

This is why most organizational changes occur when there is a change of the corporate guard. In fact, the principal reason for the premature (enforced) retirement of executives is the perception by corporate boards of the need for change.

Unfortunately, it usually requires less effort to keep an executive who will do further harm than to hire one who will do some good.

2. Knowledge is of two types, explicit and implicit, and knowing this is implicit.

Explicit knowledge is knowledge that can be consciously captured in manuals, procedural protocols, drawings and plans, and all other codified systems that help in running a business and living our lives. However necessary such knowledge may be it is not sufficient for surviving, let alone thriving. Implicit (or tacit) knowledge is also required.

Implicit knowledge is what individuals and organizations know how to do without thinking. It is done unconsciously. They may be unaware of it or, if aware, may not be able to articulate it, for example, how to ride a bicycle, run, read and write.

The things we do without thinking are more responsible for our survival and welfare than those things we do consciously and deliberately. An objective observer of how we speak, for example, may point out that we use the words "you know" as a type of punctuation. We were not aware of this. But now that we have been made aware of it, we can improve our oral delivery. It is exactly this type of objective observation of what is done unconsciously that a good consultant can bring to an organization's consciousness.

For example, in meetings, the participants almost always wait until the most senior member of the group speaks. Then those who follow tend not to disagree strongly with the opinion expressed. Because of this, viable alternatives may not be considered. By raising this practice to consciousness the habit can be revoked and more significant choices can be considered and made.

3. You rarely improve an organization as a whole by improving the performance of one or more of its parts.

An organization is a system and the performance of a system depends more on how its parts interact than on how they act when taken separately. Suppose the automobile with the best motor is identified, then the one with the best transmission, and so on for each part that an automobile requires. Suppose further that these parts are removed from the cars of which they are a part. Finally, these best parts are assembled into an automobile. We would not get the best possible car; in fact, we would not even get a car because the parts would not fit together, let alone work well together.

Similarly, if each part of a corporation is improved, it does not follow that the organization as a whole will be improved. By improving parts separately, the whole can be put out of business. Evaluation of the performance of parts of an organization should be based first on their effects on the whole, secondly on their individual performance.

In some cases the organizational performance can be improved by reducing the performance of one of its parts: by increasing inventories fewer sales may be lost because of stock shortages. The profit obtained from the otherwise lost sales may be greater than the costs associated with increased inventory. Likewise, loss leaders are products sold at a loss in order to induce additional sales of profitable products.

4. There is no point in asking consumers – who do not know what they want – to say what they want.

Many new product and service introductions have been disastrous despite the extensive surveys conducted to show that there is consumer interest in, and intention to buy, such a product or service. These surveys have incorrectly assumed that most consumers know what they want.

Consumers can discover what they want in products and services by designing them. It is in design that people find what they want. Furthermore, consumer involvement in product/service design almost always gets creative results.

Two examples:

⋄ A group of men designing their ideal men's store found that they did not want the lowest price for clothing of a specified quality but the highest quality for a specified price. (They decided how much they were going to spend before going shopping.) They also wanted clothing arranged by size not type so they could go to one part of a store where all clothing in their size was gathered. (Because they disliked shopping, they waited until they wanted to buy several things before going shopping.) They also wanted saleswomen, not men, because they said, "You can't trust a man's opinion of how you look." Finally, they wanted sales personnel to be available only when asked for.

⋄ A group of airline passengers playing with a mock-up of an airplane's interior found out how to arrange the seats so each one was on an aisle, and do so without decreasing the number of seats or increasing the number of aisles.

5. All managers believe they can do their boss's job better than their boss can, but they forget that their subordinates share the same belief about themselves.

This f/law and the difference between the salaries of different ranks are responsible for the fact that managers find it easier to look up than down. This enables them to see who is standing on their shoulders but not those on whose shoulders they are standing.

Managers have yet to learn that it is futile to supervise subordinates who know how to do their jobs better than their managers can. Fortunately, smart subordinates can conceal their bosses' ignorance even from their bosses who cannot hear the laughter that comes from behind their backs. Subordinates have yet to learn that no manager's job is as simple as it appears even though many of their managers *are* as simple-minded as they appear.

6. For managers the only conditions under which experience is the best teacher are ones in which no change takes place.

Change, particularly technological change, makes much of what was learned in the past irrelevant or obsolete. Learning how to drive an automobile does not equip one to pilot a space vehicle. Knowing how to work an abacus or slide rule does not equip one to operate a computer.

Experience is no longer the best teacher. Successful management of a corporation in the past provides no assurance of the ability to manage it successfully in the present or future. This is why few corporations live more than twenty years – either going out of business or merging with other corporations. Like corporations, knowledge has a decreasing life span. But unlike corporations, knowledge is easily renewable.

7. The level of conformity in an organization is in inverse proportion to its creative ability.

It is difficult, if not impossible, to regiment a creative mind. It tends to violate conventions and traditions without thinking about it. Such violations are means to an end not an end in itself. Creative people often dress peculiarly, even at work, and work at odd hours.

A creative person, unlike a drudge, cannot turn himself or herself off and on easily. Organizations that value creativity must develop tolerance for unconventional behavior. They should realize that such behavior is not a form of protest but a requirement for effective work.

An organization that cannot accommodate nonconformity will not be able to retain creative people. Conformity and convention are the enemies of creativity.

Ackoff's F/laws: The Cake

8. The best reason for recording what one thinks is to discover what one thinks and to organize it in transmittable form.

Corollary:

> The principal reason for reading what another thinks is to discover what the reader thinks.

Preparation of a document should be treated as a learning, not a teaching, experience. The amount that a document can teach its readers is proportional to the amount of learning the author experienced in preparing it.

There is nothing capable of being understood that cannot be expressed in ordinary English. Documents that are not written in ordinary English are not understood even by their authors.

Jargon is wool pulled over a mind to conceal that mind's ignorance from itself.

Unfortunately, obscurity is no protection against plagiarism, nor is ignorance.

9. No corporation should retain a business unit that is worth more outside the corporation than within it.

Corporations are supposed to create wealth. To retain an organization that would be worth more on the outside is to destroy wealth, not create it. The only justification for a corporation's owning a business unit lies in the value the corporation adds to that unit – not *vice versa*. If it fails to add value to the unit or it adds less than others can, the corporation does society a disservice by retaining it.

Parts of a corporation should be free to emigrate, and should be encouraged to do so, when they believe that doing so would increase their value. The existence of such a right would make corporations more aware of their responsibility to increase the value of their parts to others if not to themselves.

The right to emigrate is the most important freedom an individual or organization can have. It provides the strongest incentive for preserving the other rights that define freedom.

Ackoff's F/laws: The Cake

10. The amount of irrationality that executives attribute to others is directly proportional to their own.

Executives almost always consider themselves to be rational. But they tend to consider all those who disagree with them on any issue to be irrational. This is irrational.

For example, executives of a foundation that supported family planning efforts in developing countries considered the large number of children produced per family in these countries to be irrational. But few of these countries provided any form of social security; therefore one could only survive the unemployment that inevitably came with age if one had enough children to provide financial support. To try to convince those with no access to social security and insufficient income to support themselves, to have fewer children is to ask them to commit a delayed suicide. Now who is irrational?

In an organization, problems created by the behavior of others cannot be solved by assuming them to be irrational. They can only be solved by assuming the others to be rational, finding the point of view that makes them so, and addressing it.

The first detergent on the market failed despite its superior cleaning power. Attributing this to the irrationality of the housewife led nowhere. But assuming she was rational led to finding that she estimated the cleaning power of a product by the amount of suds it produced. The original detergent produced no suds. *Tide* then came onto the market producing suds and success.

11. The future is better dealt with using assumptions than forecasts.

Forecasts are about probabilities; assumptions are about possibilities. We carry a spare tire in our cars not because we forecast that we will have a puncture on our next trip but because we assume that a flat tire is possible. We plan for serious contingencies – floods, hurricanes, illness – however unlikely they may be.

Carrying a spare tire cannot prevent our having a flat tire but it can reduce its undesirable effect; for example, being stranded on a remote highway at night in the rain.

Of course there are futures that cannot be anticipated. These can't be planned for but they can best be met by flexible organizations, ones that can quickly detect the need to change, and are ready, willing and able to do so. For example, the driver of an automobile cannot predict all the conditions he or she will meet on the road but his or her ability to respond quickly and effectively removes the need to do so.

There is nothing that reduces the need to anticipate the future as much as the ability to respond rapidly and effectively to whatever it turns out to be.

The thermostat that controls the heating-cooling system in a building does not have to predict future weather in order to control it.

12. An organization's planning horizon is the same as its CEO's retirement horizon.

The shorter the time to retirement of an organization's CEO the more it focuses on the short run and the less on the long run. In other words, an organization's planning horizon approaches zero along with the tenure of its CEO. It then takes a quantum leap when a successor comes on board.

Most executives care more about preserving their reputations after their retirement than about the preservation of the organizations from which they retire. If, subsequently, their previous organization suffers it can always be blamed on their successors. No executives want to bequeath to their successors the opportunity to take credit for what they have done. But they want their successors to take the blame for any problems they may have passed on to them.

Successors, on the other hand, want to attribute blame to their predecessors for any problems they cannot deal with effectively. Nowhere is this more apparent than in the presidency of the USA.

13. The lower the rank of managers, the more they know about fewer things. The higher the rank of managers, the less they know about many things.

Executives make mountains out of molehills; subordinates make molehills out of mountains. Subordinates are occupied with tearing down what subordinates are building up.

The relationship between executives and subordinates is complementary: neither knows why the other does what they do; nor do they care about it.

This leaves a large black hole between them into which most important issues and communications fall – lost and, like Clementine, gone forever.

14. The importance of executives is directly proportional to the size of their waiting rooms and the number of intervening secretaries.

Arrival at the executive's waiting room is only the first step in a fruitless process. Nothing is provided to keep one productively occupied while waiting. The higher the rank of the executive, the older and less attractive the intervening secretaries are. They form the Maginot Line that can only be breached by an armored vehicle. It is one of these amazons who eventually notifies the caller that the sought-for executive has been called off on an emergency. He/she has escaped through a door not visible from the waiting room. It is not known when he or she will return.

Rain checks are not available because the executive's calendar is filled for the next month. With a smile on her face for the first time, the secretary advises, "Call again next month for an appointment."

15. When managers say something is obvious, it does not mean that it is unquestionably right, but rather that they are unwilling to have it questioned.

What managers call "obvious" may not be self-evident, not even evident to themselves. It is what they wish everyone else would accept as evident without further discussion.

The more obviously true a belief is thought to be, the more reluctance there is to discuss it, and the less willingness there is to modify it in light of whatever discussion of it takes place. "Obvious" does not mean "apparent," but "resistant to doubt."

Beware of the obvious; it is the antidote to curiosity – without which there is no creativity.

That which is apparently obvious is often wrong, but this is seldom obvious; for example, the once widely held belief that the earth is flat. There are few mental exercises more intellectually rewarding than questioning the obvious. However, doing so can be dangerous physically, as Bruno and Galileo learned.

Ackoff's F/laws: The Cake

16. The less sure managers are of their opinions, the more vigorously they defend them.

Managers do not waste their time defending beliefs they hold strongly – they just assert them. Nor do they bother to refute what they strongly believe is false. For example, they would not defend the statement, "It is necessary for the company to make a profit." Nor would they refute the statement, "It is not necessary for the company to make a profit." To most managers the former statement is obviously true and the latter obviously false, hence neither requires defense.

Managers consider it futile to argue with those who do not accept what they consider to be obvious. But if an opinion they hold but are not certain of is attacked, they leap to its defense; for example, "Downsizing is necessary for corporate survival."

It follows from this that a heresy is punished severely only when it involves beliefs that cannot be proven to be either true or false. Religion harbors the largest number of such beliefs. This is why religions experience more heresy than any other social institution. Management handles heretics more humanely than religious institutions. It does not burn them; it fires them.

17. The more lawyers an organization employs, the less innovation it tolerates.

An executive, who was not in jail at the time, once asked a retired professor of law why, whenever he asked his corporate lawyers whether he could do something new, they always said, "No." The professor replied that the executive deserved such an answer because he was asking a stupid question. The executive was shocked by this reply and said he did not understand. The ex-professor of law went on to explain. "A principal responsibility of your corporate lawyers is to keep you out of jail. You are out of jail when you ask if you can do something new. Whatever you are doing when you ask the question is apparently safe; therefore, no risk of jail is involved in no change. But doing anything differently could involve a risk, however small. Hence the lawyers' 'No.'"

"Then what," asked the executive, "should I ask?" "Don't ask anything," the retired law professor said. "Tell them what you are going to do and remind them that it is their job to keep you out of jail when you do it." Permission is almost always harder to obtain than forgiveness.

18. Good teachers produce skeptics who seek questions; management gurus produce only disciples, who seek answers.

Gurus produce disciples who disseminate without modification the doctrines they provide. Therefore, they put an end to the felt need to learn more. No disciple ever knew more than the guru who indoctrinated him or her.

On the other hand, good educators encourage others to develop ideas that are better than the ones they, the educators, present to them. Good educators produce students who know more than the educators themselves do. Good educators produce skeptics by focusing on unanswered questions and unsolved problems, and encourage them to seek answers and solutions. Educators hope to produce students who will lead, not follow.

Gurus do not educate, they indoctrinate. They provide answers, not questions or problems. They produce gospels and apostles, followers and believers, and often fanatics. Fanatics consider only a limited number of questions to be legitimate; these are the questions to which they believe they have been provided with absolutely correct answers. All other questions are considered to be unworthy of answering.

Management gurus peddle panaceas, simple solutions to complex problems. The only consultants more harmful are those who peddle complex solutions to simple problems.

19. The only thing more difficult than starting something new in an organization is stopping something old.

The momentum of an organizational practice is proportional to its age. Practices are harder to stop the older they are. Innovations have no age, hence no momentum, and therefore are easy to stop.

As Ambrose Bierce, the great American wit, noted, there is an infinite number of reasons for not doing something, but only one for doing it: it is the right thing to do. But this is very hard to prove.

This is why, for example, old generals do not die; they fade away slowly while serving as experts on television. Retired executives and generals become experts when they are freed of responsibility for their opinions. It is amazing how capable retired generals and executives become in solving the problems they could not solve before they retired.

20. Acceptance of a recommended solution to a problem depends more on the manager's trust of its source than on the content of the recommendation or the competence of its source.

One who receives a recommendation can never share the entire process that led up to it. It is always possible that there is an undetected aspect of the recommendation that could harm the recipient, even if unintentionally. For this reason, the more the recipient trusts the one making the recommendation, the more likely it is to be accepted.

No amount of competence can compensate for a lack of trust. Friendship is an ultimate act of trust; therefore, it is the advice of friends, however bad, not that of enemies, however good, that is most likely to be followed.

Friends are ones who can be trusted to make decisions in our best interest even when doing so involves sacrificing their own. A friend always tries to do what is perceived as best for us, which is something we do not do for ourselves.

It is much easier for an organization to protect itself against an enemy's conscious efforts to harm it than to protect itself against harmful acts done unconsciously by friends. Well-intentioned acts based on ignorance can do more harm than badly intentioned acts based on knowledge. Ignorance is a much more serious enemy than ill will.

21. The less managers understand their business, the more variables they require to explain it.

$E = mc^2$ (the special theory of relativity) contains only one independent variable, *m*, and explains what may well be the most complicated phenomena understood by scientists. Then why does it take thirty-five variables to understand why people select the retail store or the cereal they use? The answer is apparent: these phenomena are *not* understood. The less something is understood, the more variables are required to provide an alleged explanation of it.

Understanding provides managers with a way of determining the relevance of information. This is why managers who do not understand what is happening want all the information about it that they can get. Not knowing what information is relevant, they fear omitting anything that *might* be relevant. Consequently, they suffer much more from an oversupply of irrelevant information than from a shortage of relevant information. Good managers are eventually able to sort out the relevant information and discard the irrelevant.

Ackoff's F/laws: The Cake

22. The higher the rank of managers, the less is the distance between their offices and their restrooms.

Corollary 1:

The distance between offices is directly proportional to the difference between the ranks of their occupants.

Corollary 2:

The higher a manager's rank, the less distance there is between his/her office and his/her parking space.

The principal privilege enjoyed by those of high rank is minimization of the distances they must walk. Their restrooms are normally located adjacent to their offices or within them. For some executives their restrooms are their offices.

It is considered demeaning for one of high rank to walk to the office of a subordinate or to another floor of the headquarters building (other than the floor containing the executive dining room or barber). This all follows from the assumption that the length of executives' legs is inversely proportional to the circumference of their rank.

"Walk the talk" is futile advice to executives because for them walking and talking are incompatible activities. They can do only one at a time. Therefore, they choose to talk. It takes less effort and thought.

23. Business schools are as difficult to change as cemeteries, and for the same reasons.

Tenure anesthetizes the minds of most faculty members, as much as job security anesthetizes the minds of those executives who enjoy it; it produces a complacency that encourages early retirement of the mind. There is no better guarantee of security than increasing competence, and none that discourages such increase more than tenure.

In the first half of the twentieth century tenure was seldom granted to a faculty member before the age of fifty. Therefore, the decision to grant it was based on performance over twenty-five to thirty years, and an expectation of continued productivity over no more than the next ten to fifteen years. Today, tenure is usually granted in the early thirties. This means it is often based on a very few years of teaching and research, and also on a projection of continued productivity over thirty to forty years. Little wonder that these projections are so frequently wrong.

There are better ways of protecting academic freedom than tenure, but no better way of protecting incompetence.

24. Curiosity is the "open sesame" to learning, even for managers.

Preschoolers are curious about almost everything. Postschoolers are curious about almost nothing. They think they already know everything they need to know.

Schools, including business schools, restrict the kinds of questions that may be asked by students to ones that are not controversial and for which answers are thought to be available. Not permissible are such questions as:

- Why, in the richest country in the world, are there more than forty million people living in poverty and a similar number who have no, or inadequate, health care coverage?
- Why does the United States have the second highest percentage of its population in prison of any country and simultaneously the highest crime rate?
- Of the many gods believed in around the world, which is the most authentic and who authenticates god?
- What is life and when does it begin?

Not only are children and managers taught not to ask the right questions, but they are also taught to provide expected answers, whether right or wrong, to the wrong ones. Advancement depends on it, in school and later in business. Creativity is killed in those restricted to asking expected questions and providing expected answers.

Effective leadership or management is not possible without creativity, but administration, which is frequently mistaken for both, *is* possible without creativity.

25. The legibility of a male manager's handwriting is in inverse proportion to his seniority.

The less legible a male manager's signature is, the higher his rank and the more education he has had.

Female managers are genetically incapable of writing illegibly unless they are physicians. The illegibility of physicians' handwriting is the standard to which all other professionals, including managers, aspire. Illegibility of prescriptions prepared by doctors is responsible for the requirement imposed on pharmacists that they become psychics capable of reading the minds of physicians. The illegibility of handwritten memos from executives is similarly responsible for a similar requirement imposed on their secretaries.

Those managers who have not learned how to write illegibly can nevertheless accomplish the same thing by resorting to obscurity. Computers may help reduce illegibility but they have no effect on obscurity.

The illegible and obscure writings of managers hide what they know (if anything). The illegible and obscure writings of management educators hide what they don't know.

26. Executives must be prevented from receiving any information about frauds or immoral acts committed by their subordinates.

This is referred to as the principle of blissful ignorance. The principle works both ways, symmetrically. Subordinates are not supposed to know about any illegal or immoral acts committed by their superiors. In both cases this leaves very little for them to know.

27. There is nothing that a manager wants done that educated subordinates cannot undo.

The basis of this f/law is as follows: the more *power-over* educated subordinates that managers exercise, the less is their *power-to* get them to do what they want them to.

Power-over is the ability to reward or punish subordinates for meeting or missing their boss's expectations. Power-to is the ability to induce them to do willingly what the boss wants them to. Therefore, the ultimate source of power-over is physical or economic, but the ultimate source of power-to is intelligence.

The effectiveness of power-over decreases as the educational level of subordinates increases. It becomes negative when the educational level of the subordinates is higher than that of their bosses.

The exercise of authority is necessary for getting a job done by those who do not know how to do it, as, for example, in using aborigines to build a concrete house. For those who know how to do it, the intervention of authority is an obstruction to getting it done, as, for example, in telling a plumber how to fix a leak.

28. The more corporate executives believe in a free (unregulated) external market, the more they believe in a regulated internal market.

Internal service and supply units are seldom required to compete against external sources or each other for both internal and external business. If they were required to do so, this would prevent bloating, the creation of "make work," and eliminate a major source of the need for "rightsizing."

Unfortunately, managers who vigorously oppose the regulation of business by government, vigorously regulate the parts of their own businesses. Most enterprises operate with the same kind of centrally planned and controlled economy as was used in the Soviet Union.

Perestroika, the replacement of a centrally controlled economy by a market economy, is as relevant to Western corporations as it was to the Soviet Union.

29. The amount of time a committee wastes is directly proportional to its size.

The amount of useful output generated by a committee decreases as its size increases. Therefore, the optimal size of a committee is zero or less. Committee meetings are a very efficient way of sharing ignorance and prejudices.

The function of committees is not to make decisions but to delay their being made long enough to allow the issue involved to fade away. A committee is an instrument for managing by default.

The value of a committee is judged to be proportional to the length of time and amount of money it requires to come to no conclusion, and the length of the report on the way it got there. The length of the report is inversely related to the amount of information it contains.

Those who convene committee meetings (or any meetings) should be required to pay for the time of those who attend. This would not only make meetings more productive but it would reduce their number and duration.

30. It is generally easier to evaluate an organization from the outside-in than from the inside-out.

One of the principal reasons given by an organization for rejecting changes suggested by outsiders is their alleged lack of familiarity with the organization involved.

A change in the operations of a railroad was once suggested to an elderly railroad executive who then asked if the man proposing the change had ever worked on a railroad. He said no. The elderly executive then asked if his father had ever worked on a railroad. Again he said no. The executive then asked if anyone in his family had ever worked on a railroad. The answer was still no. Then he asked why the one making the suggestion thought he was qualified to suggest how to operate a railroad. He replied by telling the executive a story that he had heard attributed to the architectural critic, Lewis Mumford. When Mumford was asked what right he had to criticize an architectural design, never having prepared one himself, he is alleged to have said, "I have never laid an egg but I know the difference between a good and a bad one."

The railroad executive was completely unfazed by this story. He said, "I was talking about railroads, not eggs." To say of some executives that they are dense is to say that their minds are very difficult to penetrate.

31. Development is less about how much an organization has than how much it can do with whatever it has.

How much an individual or organization has is largely a matter of wealth: how much has been *earned* or otherwise acquired. Standard of living is an index of wealth. How much one can do with whatever one has is a matter of competence: how much has been *learned*. It is reflected in the quality of life achieved.

The more developed individuals or organizations are, the less wealth they require to obtain a satisfactory quality of life. Equally, the more developed individuals or organizations are, the better the quality of life they can obtain with whatever wealth they have. A small, developed organization can provide a better quality of work life than a less developed one that is richer and larger.

Robinson Crusoe is a much better model of development than J. Pierpont Morgan, Commodore Vanderbilt, or John D. Rockefeller. There are few organizations in which development is valued as much as, let alone more than, growth. A preoccupation with growth in an individual is pathological but it is generally considered to be healthy in organizations.

32. Smart subordinates can make their managers look bad no matter how good they are, and make their managers look good no matter how bad they are.

The performance of managers depends more on their subordinates' performance than it does on their own, but their subordinates' performance depends little on that of their superiors.

A group of highly trained graduates often know more about their work than their bosses do. In addition, they know that they know more, and that their bosses don't know this, and they break rules for which they know they can't be fired because their bosses' jobs depend on their performance. Hence, they may come to work in jeans, work odd hours, keep messy desks, and talk a lot to each other. This distracts their bosses but they know which side their butter is breaded on.

Therefore, a successful manager of highly educated subordinates is one who enables them to do whatever they want to do providing they also do the job the manager wants them to do.

33. In an organization that disapproves of mistakes, but identifies only errors of commission, the best strategy for anyone who seeks job security is to do nothing.

This more than anything explains corporate resistance to change. Not changing threatens survival much more often than changing. In a turbulent environment it is usually better to do something than nothing. The only equilibrium that can be found when flying through a storm is dynamic.

The metaphor that is often invoked is to "keep your head down." Otherwise, obviously, it can be shot off as punishment for a mistake. While individual managers may temporarily survive using this tactic, the organization's survival may be threatened by the failure to act in times of change.

An organization that always punishes mistakes risks meeting a future over which it has no control because managers were afraid to advocate changes that might avert future crises. A tolerance for mistakes can enable an organization to have a major role in creating its future.

One corporation distributed this statement to its managers: "If you didn't make a serious mistake last year, you didn't do your job; you didn't try something new. But if you make the same mistake next year, you won't be here the following year." In effect, this says that making a mistake is forgivable but only if learning results from it.

Ackoff's F/laws: The Cake

34. The best organizational designers are ones who know how to beat any organization designed by others.

The better a system designer is at beating systems the more likely he or she is to design a system that is difficult to beat. Some systems are foolproof, but there are none that are proof against smart people. No one can design an organization that someone else cannot beat, especially if they have the help of lawyers. No lawyer ever wrote a law or regulation that precluded other lawyers from making a living out of beating it. For every organization there is a lawyer somewhere who can beat it by hook or crook, especially crook.

Contrary to popular belief, even government-imposed constraints and restrictions can be beaten, especially with the help of lobbyists who are lawyers in disguise.

A business-school course on "How to beat systems" would be the most valuable course a future manager could take. It is not offered because what would be learned in such a course could be turned against the school in which it was learned. There are few systems that are as worthy of being beaten.

35. The offense taken by an organization from negative press is directly proportional to its truthfulness.

Nothing can offend an organization more than the truth about itself. It is easy for it to defend itself against lies but very difficult to do so against truths. This is why so many organizations would rather settle suits out of court; doing so conceals truths. The rationalizations given seldom reflect this fact.

What organizations seek from others, including the press, is reinforcement of the delusions they have about themselves. They never see themselves as others do, nor do they see others as they do. The result is an equitable distribution of distortion.

36. The less important an issue is, the more time managers spend discussing it.

More time is spent on small talk than is spent on large talk. Most talk is about what matters least. What matters least is what most of us know most about. The more something matters, the less we are likely to know about it.

Everyone is an expert on trivia. So everyone can discuss trivialities with equal authority and at great length. This is not true with important issues on which there are alleged experts. Experts – those who know a great deal about a subject – tend to limit discussion to what they know about it. Their authority is vulnerable to new ideas, which, of course, seldom come from other experts, but from non-experts whom experts try to exclude from the discussion.

Experts seldom accept any responsibility for errors resulting from following their advice. However, they accept full responsibility for any successes that result from following their advice, however remote the connection.

37. The time spent waiting to get into an executive's office is directly proportional to the difference in rank between the executive and the one waiting to get in.

A caller of higher rank than the executive is shown in at once even if it means waking him up.

Alcoholic beverages are offered to those of higher rank when they enter. Coffee is offered to those of the same rank as the executive whose office it is. Nothing is offered to those of lower rank. Those of the lowest rank are not seated.

38. Administration, management and leadership are not the same thing.

Administration is the direction of others in the pursuit of ends and by the use of means both selected by others.

Management is the direction of others in the pursuit of ends and by the use of means selected by a manager.

Leadership is the direction of others in the pursuit of ends and by the use of means collectively selected by those involved.

Those who follow a leader do so voluntarily. He/she takes them where they want to go. Leaders do not exercise authority over followers; managers do. Those who command and control do not lead; they manage.

39. **In acquisitions the value added to the acquired company is much more important than the value added to the acquiring company.**

The price required to acquire a company is almost always greater than it is currently worth. Therefore, it is important for the potential acquirer to estimate how much value it can add to the acquired company. How much would the acquired company be worth taking this added value into account?

The reason that most acquisitions do not turn out to be successful is that the value of the acquired company decreases after the acquisition. This, in turn, reduces the value of the acquiring company.

Due diligence at best reveals the current value of an acquisition candidate. Diligent planning of how to enhance its value is required. Such planning is the most diligent thing a potential acquirer can do.

40. Business schools are high security prisons of the mind.

Business schools restrict or deny freedom of choice. They specify what must be taught, and when and how. What is scheduled is teaching, not learning.

Under the pretext of evaluating students, business schools prohibit "cheating" by making minds work in solitary confinement. When taking examinations or preparing work, collaboration is a no-no. But once students enter the *real* world, what was taken to be cheating in school becomes highly valued collaboration with others in the quest for understanding. Business schools discourage learning from others even though it is the principal way that graduates will learn for the rest of their lives.

Managers are not evaluated by what they can accomplish without help but by what they can accomplish with all the help they can garner. How to use others effectively is one of the most important things a student of management can learn, but it is a dangerous thing to try to learn in a business school.

Faculty members do not motivate students to want to continue after their schooling is complete. They remove the perceived need for any further learning by pretending to provide students with all the answers the faculty thinks they will ever need. Faculty members' perception of what their students will need after graduation is rarely tainted by any contact with reality.

41. No matter how large and successful an organization is, if it fails to adapt to change, then, like a dinosaur, it will become extinct.

To determine how an organization would destroy itself by not adapting to change requires determining the future "it is now in." This is the future it would have if it were to continue its current behavior and the environment were to change only as expected. The future based on these assumptions, both false, is then projected out to the organization's inevitable self-destruction.

Self-destruction is inevitable on this basis because the organization would not adapt to even expected changes in its environment. The point is to reveal the Achilles heel of the organization, the source of its potential self-destruction. It also suggests how such self-destruction can be avoided.

In the 1970s such a projection revealed that, should the Federal Reserve Bank continue to clear checks in the same way, the number of check clearers eventually required would exceed the number of people living in the United States. Such a situation obviously had to be avoided. But it could be avoided either by what was done to the bank or by what the bank did. By taking the initiative, the FRB created its own future. It initiated development of the electronic fund transfer system, which reduced the rate of increase in the number of checks per year and eventually their absolute number.

42. The size of a CEO's bonus is directly proportional to how much more the company would have lost had it not been for him or her.

Corollary:

The size of a CEO's bonus is also directly proportional to:

(a) the number of people he/she has laid off and

(b) his/her responsibility for the apparent need to do so.

A company's increase in stock price after downsizing is proportional to the number of people laid off, providing none of them are executives. As most executives have learned, they can increase their bonus further by leaving the company after selling it or having assured its demise.

The demise of a company is always attributed to external – never internal – conditions it could not control. The national economy is always available to be blamed, as is unfair (and possibly illegal) competition. Mistakes that can't be accounted for in this way can be attributed to the irrational behavior of employees (especially if unionized), suppliers or customers.

Executives can never be held responsible for mistakes they make, but with great difficulty they can be held responsible for mistakes their subordinates make, mistakes of which they claim to have been completely unaware, especially if they were illegal.

43. The less managers expect of their subordinates, the less they get.

Most of our expectations of others and ourselves are self-fulfilling prophecies. For example, teachers learn early that if they expect students to cheat, their students will not disappoint them. They will go to extremes to meet their teachers' expectations.

Children try hard to meet their parents' expectations no matter how unreasonable they are. The same is true of subordinates of managers. Managers try to lower the expectations that their superiors have of them in order to appear to be performing above expectations. The result: lower expectations and lower performance.

44. The amount of money spent to broadcast a television or radio commercial is inversely related to its truthfulness and relevance.

There should be a law that enables class action suits to be filed against advertisers who make false or misleading claims. There isn't such a law because elimination of such claims would put most media out of business. Furthermore, there are not enough courts and judges to handle the caseload that would result. But there are enough lawyers. Suing false claimers would provide lawyers with something socially useful to do. No wonder they do not do it!

The only commercials that avoid misleading the viewers or listeners are those that leave them wondering what product or service is being advertised. However, even bad television commercials provide intermissions that can be useful biologically. How much better such breaks would be if only the benefactor was identified and not his or her product or service. The absence of truth in TV advertising is not nearly as important as its lack of relevance.

45. The more managers focus on how hard their subordinates work, to the exclusion of how much they play, learn and are inspired on the job, the less productive their work is likely to be.

In the Renaissance, human activities were dissected into four categories: work, play, learning, and inspiration. The West then developed institutions where each of these could be engaged in to the exclusion of the others. Factories and business offices, for example, are designed for work, not for learning, fun, or inspiration. Country clubs are designed to provide fun, not work, learning, or inspiration. Museums and churches provide learning and inspiration but neither of the other two. Schools provide learning, but none of the other three.

The effectiveness of an activity and the joy that can be derived from it depends on the extent to which all four of these aspects of life are integrated. Therefore, ideal corporations, country clubs, schools, and museums would be distinguishable from each other only by their emphasis.

A few such corporations exist; very few.

46. A bureaucrat is one who has the power to say "no" but none to say "yes."

Bureaucrats can find an infinite number of reasons for rejecting any proposed change, but can find none for accepting it. Since they cannot say "yes," if they want to have a proposal accepted, they must pass it on to someone of higher rank. But to do this is to acknowledge a limit to their importance and, therefore, to lose face. Their self-esteem is directly proportional to the number of times they say "no," and inversely proportional to the number of times they say "yes."

In a bureaucracy a "no" cannot lead to what is considered to be an error, only a "yes" can do that. Therefore, within a bureaucracy, doing as little as possible is the best strategy for avoiding detectable errors.

47. Teleconferencing is an electronic way of wasting more time than is saved in travel.

When one's attendance at a meeting is electronic, one cannot feel as much a part of it as when one is present. It is psychologically uncomfortable because body language is one of the most important forms of communication. This tends to make the meetings less participative and productive than those held in a conference room.

Unfortunately, the ease with which teleconferences can be set up is an incentive to hold more of them than are actually needed. Such meetings are interpreted as evidence that an organization is "with" new technology, rather than more productive.

48. The more important the problem that a manager asks consultants for help on, the less useful and more costly their solutions are likely to be.

Consultants begin their engagements by gathering very large amounts of data – much more than can be transformed into useful information. No wonder! Their fees are proportional to the amount of time they devote to a problem, not to the amount of good that they do.

The most successful consultants are the ones who are smart enough to see what managers want and give it to them after an extended effort, and do so in long, impressively formatted reports. They provide sanctions for a fee.

The principal finding obtained by all studies conducted by consultants, regardless of the issues involved, is the need for more study. The success of a consultant's effort is not measured by the amount of good it does for the client, but the amount of good it does for the consultant.

49. The distance between managers' offices is directly proportional to the difference between the ranks of their occupants.

Executives of the same rank have unconnected offices next to each other. This enables their secretaries to control access to their bosses, even by their peers. Their superiors do not come to their offices; they go to those of their superiors.

Subordinates who call are prioritized and stored in the waiting room for future reference.

Ackoff's F/laws: The Cake

50. The *sine qua non* of leadership is talent, and talent cannot be taught.

One can be taught to draw but one cannot be taught to be an artist. The difference is talent, a gift at birth. One's talent can be enhanced. Tools and techniques can be transmitted to artists as well as to draftsmen. The essential requirement of a leader is an ability to inspire. Inspiration is an art, not a science. Leadership, then, is more an art than a science.

Leadership development courses and programs can develop those who already have the requisite talent but they cannot make leaders out of those who are without it. What such courses and programs do and do very well is make managers who cannot lead think they can.

51. Managers who don't know how to measure what they want settle for wanting what they can measure.

For example, those who want a high quality of work life but don't know how to measure it, often settle for wanting a high standard of living because they can measure it. The tragedy is that they come to believe that quality of life and standard of living are the same thing. The fact is that further increases to an already high standard of living often reduce quality of life.

Unfortunately and similarly, the (unmeasurable) quality of products or services is taken to be proportional to their (measurable) price. The price of a product or service, however, is usually proportional to the cost of producing it, not to its quality; and this cost tends to be proportional to the relative incompetence of the organization that produces it.

Like economists, managers place no value on work they do not pay for because they can't measure it. Work that has no quantifiable output includes some of the most important work that is done, for example, raising children and maintaining a home. On the other hand, economists place a high value on work that destroys value, because the cost of such work can be measured. Hence the paradox: a prolonged war is a very good way of raising gross national product but also of reducing quality of life.

52. A great big happy family requires more loyalty than competence, but a great big happy business requires more competence than loyalty.

Loyalty is much more important for the preservation of a family than for the preservation of a business. Allocating authority and responsibility in a family business on the basis of competence may well destroy the family but preserve the business.

In a family, the weakest members usually receive the most care, attention, and resources. When carried over to a business this is a recipe for failure.

It is often better to pay a member of the family to stay away from the business than to pay them for becoming a part of it.

53. If an organization must grow, it is better for it to grow horizontally than vertically.

Horizontal growth of organizations widens management's spans of control but retains the same number of layers. The more layers there are, the more difficult it is to integrate vertical interactions. The wider the spans of control, the easier it is to coordinate horizontal interactions.

The spans of control of managers in the United States are generally much too narrow. This results in an excess of managers. The excess derives from the fact that in order to increase deserving employees' salaries beyond the maximum allowable for those of their rank, they must be promoted to a managerial position for which there is no need. If salaries were based on performance, not on rank or category, the surplus of managers would be reduced, spans of control widened, and layers decreased. Performance would increase.

American corporations – unlike most of their executives – have a profile like an hourglass: large spans of control at the top and bottom, and small spans in the middle.

The greater the excess of managers in the middle, the harder it is for the top and bottom to communicate with each other.

54. **Corporate development and corporate growth are not the same thing and neither requires the other.**

Cemeteries and rubbish heaps grow but do not develop; Einstein continued to develop without growing; in fact, he contracted as he aged. This is true of corporations too: they can grow without developing and develop without growing.

Growth is an increase in size or number. Development is an increase in competence, in one's ability to satisfy one's own needs and legitimate desires, and those of others. A legitimate desire is one the satisfaction of which does not decrease anyone else's ability or desire to satisfy their own needs and legitimate desires.

Corpulence is a product of growth; competence a product of development. Growth is quantitative; development is qualitative. Growth is a matter of earning; development is a matter of learning. The objective of growth is to increase standard of living; the objective of development is to increase quality of life.

A corporation develops to the extent that it increases its ability to contribute to the development of its stakeholders. Growth may inhibit development but development cannot inhibit growth. Bigger is not necessarily better. The best reason a corporation can have for growing is to maintain or increase employment while increasing the productivity of labor. Here growth is a means, not an end.

55. The uniqueness of an organization lies more in what it hides than what it exposes.

Public relations and corporate advertising are designed to create an illusion, a shadow that will be perceived by others as substantial. It is a product of wishful thinking. Just as the uniqueness of a person does not lie in the clothes he/she wears, the uniqueness of an organization does not lie in the words with which it dresses itself. It lies in what it does, not what it says about itself.

One can differ without being unique, especially when many others differ in the same way.

It is much easier for an organization to create a unique logo and slogan than a unique work environment or even a unique product or service. Uniqueness is seldom the result of a deliberate and conscious act. It derives from the way an organization thinks and acts. Originality is not a commodity. It cannot be acquired from others; it must be developed from within.

56. The telephone, which once facilitated communication, now increasingly obstructs it.

The telephone is now used to enable a synthetic source of speech to indicate to callers that those with whom they wish to communicate do not want to be reached. But it does give callers an opportunity to exercise their index fingers by pushing buttons before they are put on hold and subsequently cut off.

It once took only seven digits and a small amount of time to reach most people. Now the number of digits and the amount of time required have increased exponentially and exceed the capacity of a normal person's memory or patience.

The routing choices offered synthetically seldom reveal the choice one wants. This often leads to a vain effort to reach a person. In the rare case in which a person is reached, that person is unqualified to respond to the need of the caller and doesn't know who is. This initiates a series of transfers that terminates in a carefully programmed accidental cut-off.

The telephone, which once significantly reduced the need to write, is now driving us back to it. Our vocal cords are being replaced by fingers on an electronic keyboard and eyes squinting at a screen.

57. Managers cannot learn from doing things right, only from doing them wrong.

Doing something right can only confirm what one already knows or believes; one cannot learn from it. However, one can learn from making mistakes, by identifying and correcting them. Nevertheless, making a mistake is frowned upon in most organizations, from school on up, and is often punishable. To the extent that recognition of mistakes is suppressed, so is learning.

There are two types of mistakes. Errors of commission consist of doing something that *should not* have been done. Errors of omission consist of not doing something that *should* have been done. Errors of omission are more serious than errors of commission because, among other reasons, they are often impossible or very difficult to correct. They are lost opportunities that can never be retrieved.

58. The principal objective of corporate executives is to provide themselves with the standard of living and quality of work life to which they aspire.

Accountability is the price managers are supposed to pay for getting what they want out of their employment. Like all prices, they try to minimize it. They often succeed by passing it on to their subordinates who in turn pass it on to their subordinates until it passes out of the system. Accountability, unlike the buck, stops nowhere.

Maximization of shareholder value is alleged to be the principal objective of corporations. This illusion, propagated by executives, makes it possible to conceal their real objective: sustainable privilege.

Profit is a requirement, not an objective. As Peter Drucker once pointed out, profit is to a corporation what oxygen is to a human being: necessary for its existence, not a reason for it. Profit has absolutely no value to a corporation until it gets rid of it. This is also the case with many executives.

59. The principal obstruction to an organization getting to where its managers most want it to be lies in the minds of its managers.

One can easily excuse oneself for not trying to get to where one wants to be: "They (or it) won't let me." Such attributions of blame are usually self-deceptions. The great American philosopher Pogo revealed the truth when he said, "We have met the enemy and he is us."

The fear of losing one's security and lack of self-confidence are the principal obstructions to progress – in other words, risk aversion. This lies inside, not outside, managers. There is no obstruction harder to recognize, let alone evade, than one that lies within oneself, largely because the content of one's mind is usually not visible to oneself.

In a changing environment, the future of an organization is generally determined more by what its management fails to do than by what it does. Organizational futures, or the lack thereof, are more often created by default than by deliberation.

60. A corporation's external boundaries are generally much more penetrable than its internal ones.

The competition for personal power and resources between managers and units within a corporation is often much more intense and less ethical than competition between corporations for customers.

Many managers act as though their performance, and hence their bonus, depends more on what their peers within the organization do, than on what their counterparts in other organizations do. And they believe their peers are "out to get them." Therefore, the information flow between peers is often less than it is between counterparts.

Improving communication between competing managers can often make things worse. Equally, with no information flowing between peers, the intensity of conflict between them decreases, but, unfortunately, so does organizational performance.

61. It is very difficult for those inside a box to think outside of it.

Those inside an organization, like those in Plato's cave, can only see shadows of things outside the organization. In addition, unlike those in Plato's cave, they often see only shadows of things inside the organization. Shadows are two-dimensional images of multi-dimensional reality; they fail to reflect the complexity of their source.

Shadows are determined by those who cast them, not by those who see them. They cannot be manipulated, but those who try often suffer from the illusion that they can be. An organization cannot control the future, but it can control a great deal of the effect of that future upon it. The extent to which it can exercise such control depends on how well it can see the truth about itself.

It is very difficult for an organization to see the truth about itself. Those inside a box can seldom see what is happening within it. It usually takes someone looking from the outside in to produce useful evaluations.

62. The level of organizational development is directly proportional to the size of the gap between where the organization is and where it wants to be.

Those who cannot think of a better state of affairs than the one they are in have no capacity for development. The smaller the gap between where an organization is and where it wants to be, the less developed it is. For example, reactionary, narrow-minded groups often cannot imagine a life much better than the one they have (except that they would like to undo recent changes in order to revert to a "golden age"). On the other hand, well developed organizations and societies can think of many positive changes that would improve the quality of life they provide.

Continuous development requires:

◇ continuous unwillingness to settle for the state one is in however satisfying it may be

◇ a conception of a better state

◇ a way of pursuing it progressively that enables those doing so to extract satisfaction from the pursuit.

Therefore, development requires both inspiration, the stimulation that induces the pursuit of something better, and recreation, the extraction of satisfaction from the pursuit itself.

Few organizations provide either.

63. Most stated, corporate objectives are platitudes – they say nothing, but hide this fact behind words.

Many alleged statements have no content, say nothing. For example, "Too much alcohol (or anything) is bad for you." This is a platitude; perhaps the worst kind, a tautology. A tautology is a statement that asserts that something is itself. Can you imagine asserting that "Too much alcohol is good for you."? Of course not, because "too much" means "an amount that is bad for you."

Therefore, the statement "Too much alcohol is bad for you" is equivalent to "An amount of alcohol that is bad for you is bad for you." *Motherhood statements* are also platitudes. They are statements the negative of which would never be asserted by a reasonable person, let alone a manager.

For example, "We should provide our stockholders with an adequate return on their investments." Can you imagine anyone asserting that a corporation shouldn't do this? Unless the negative of an assertion is sensible, the positive version cannot be.

Most stated corporate objectives put to this test would dissolve.

64. Most corporations and business schools are less than the sum of their parts.

The break-up value of most business schools and corporations is greater than their value as a whole. This follows from the fact that one of their core competencies is their ability to prevent productive interactions between their parts. They obstruct each other and this results in negative synergy.

In corporations, as in business schools, negative synergy is a consequence of disapproval, if not punishment, of those who cross departmental lines. Those who do so are believed to be disloyal to their department and to be prostituting their competence.

The strength of an individual's loyalty is usually greatest when applied to the smallest organizational unit of which that individual is a part. It decreases as the size of the containing units increase. Thus, one's greatest loyalty is to oneself; one's smallest loyalty is to humankind.

65. Managers who try to make themselves look good by making others look bad, generally look worse than those they try to make look bad.

It is easier to make others fail than to help them succeed. Therefore, it is easier for subordinates to make their superiors fail than to help them succeed. Enmity begets enmity; cooperation begets cooperation. In order for managers to rise in a hierarchy over the remains of others, they must receive the cooperation of the others they have damaged on the way up. They are unlikely to get it.

To be elevated because of one's own competence is better than elevation because of the apparent incompetence of others. A great deal more can be accomplished with the help of competent others than with the absence of help from incompetent others. Therefore, one of the best ways for managers to help themselves is to help increase the competence of their subordinates and their peers.

66. The morality that many managers espouse in public is inversely proportional to the morality they practice in private.

Be wary of those who berate the morality of others and celebrate their own in public. One's own morality does not require reinforcement by attacking the immorality of others. Morality is its own reward; it does not require the awareness, approval, admiration, or financial support of others. Immorality does.

Those who preach virtue publicly and pretend to practice it are trying either to conceal their own sins, or to make a living off the sins of others.

Overt moralists greatly resent the fun others have from behaving immorally. Perhaps the reason they do not practice the morality they preach is that they do not know how to have fun morally.

Ackoff's F/laws: The Cake

67. The higher their rank, the less managers perceive a need for continuing education, but the greater their need for it.

The pretension to omniscience increases with rank and it does so with decreasing justification. In general, the more senior the managers, the more open their mouths and the more closed their minds.

The only way to get senior executives to attend a course is to hold it in the Bahamas on a golf course and have them bring their wives or a reasonable facsimile thereof. The educational part of a senior executive course must be restricted to no more than a few hours per day, with attendance optional. The course must also be very costly. Its value is judged to be directly proportional to its cost, its distance from home, and its exclusion of those of lower rank.

The most popular presenters are managerial evangelists and panacea peddlers. They are evaluated more by the energy they exert than the enlightenment they spread, by the excitement they induce rather than the inspiration they provide.

Unfortunately, most evangelists and panacea peddlers can propagate trivia more convincingly than most educators can transmit knowledge, understanding or wisdom.

68. **The number of references and citations in a book is inversely proportional to the amount of thinking the author has done.**

The number of citations is often used as a basis for estimating the knowledge of the author. Nothing could be a less reliable guide. The number of references and citations is directly proportional to the amount of thinking of others he/she has used. Most allegedly learned books are nothing but compilations of other people's learning, carefully organized and presented so as to be less comprehensible than the originals.

Appropriate and approved citations are what give a book legitimacy. For example, any book on management that does not cite Peter Drucker immediately brands the author as illiterate. Authors are not expected to have read Drucker but they are expected to feel guilty if they haven't.

The number of times an author refers to him/herself is proportional to the extent that the current writing repeats what he/she has previously written.

Finally, no author has ever read all the books he or she cites.

69. No computer is smarter than those who program it. Those who program computers are seldom smarter than those who try to use their output.

Therefore, the computer has become a very efficient way of distributing ignorance and inefficiency. It is extremely efficient in consuming time unproductively, but in a challenging and entertaining way. Trying to prove that a person is smarter than the computer is an entertaining way of getting nothing done.

There is only one thing a computer can do that a person can't do: remember a forecast without changing it. Of course it can do many things faster than a person, especially wrong things.

Computers cannot use people nearly as well as people can use computers. A great deal more can be done by people without computers than by computers without people. Computers amplify man's incapabilities; they do not replace them. They cannot distinguish between right and wrong, good and evil, and beauty and ugliness.

Information and knowledge can be entered into a computer, but not understanding and wisdom. However rare understanding and wisdom are among humans, they are not to be found at all in computers.

Technology is neither good nor evil, but it enhances man's inclination toward both.

Ackoff's F/laws: The Cake

70. Managers cannot talk and listen at the same time; in fact, most managers find it very difficult to listen even when they are not talking.

Some consider this to be the most serious defect possible in the design of managers. It is bad enough that they cannot hear what others are saying, but they do not even hear themselves. This prevents them from doing unto themselves as they do unto others. Managers talk to or at their subordinates to avoid having to listen to them or themselves.

Hearing and listening are not the same thing. To hear another is to know that they are saying something without knowing *what* they are saying. Knowing what they are saying requires listening. Hearing is done with the ears; listening is done with the mind; listening is minding what others have to say. One must have a mind to listen; ears are not enough.

Failure to listen results in atrophy of the mind.

71. Overheads, slides and PowerPoint projectors are not visual aids to managers. They transform managers into auditory aids to the visuals.

Black, white and green boards and easels-and-pads are visual aids, but slide, overhead and PowerPoint projectors are not. They eliminate the need for the speaker to think while talking. The speaker is frequently viewed as an obstruction to reading what is projected.

In general, the more artistic projections are, the less significant is their content. Copies of slides or overheads distributed beforehand eliminate the need for members of the audience to pay attention to the speaker and remove any guilt they might feel by not doing so. This is not altered by the fact that the handouts are seldom used after the presentation. Their principal function is to provide evidence of attendance. They also provide those in the audience with something to occupy their minds while the speaker drones on.

In addition, a speaker who reads what is on the screen insults a literate audience unless he or she had the foresight to make the projections illegible or incomprehensible.

Ackoff's F/laws: The Cake

72. Conversations in a lavatory are more productive than those in the boardroom.

An informal conversation while "using the facilities" is often more productive than a long, stifling, formal meeting. There is unlikely to be posturing or political infighting at such a time and place. And what is being passed is not the time of day.

Women managers are at a disadvantage because of the difference in the physical layout of men's and women's restrooms. This is not likely to change but women's behavior in their facilities is likely to. Perhaps installing intra-cubicle communication equipment (auditory, not visual) would help.

Women will have to learn that privacy is not nearly as important as the ability to converse without constraints.

73. In advertising, all competing products or services have a common property: each is better than all the others.

It follows that every product or service on the market is also worse than all the others.

Comparative ads are intended to support a product's claim for superiority over the one generally recognized as the best in the class. All this does is firmly establish the one considered to be the best in its class as the best in its class. No product has ever been knocked out of a leadership position by a product that claims to be better than it is, unless it is better.

Each advertiser emphasizes the positive and ignores the negative. There is no product/service that is not better than its competition relative to some property. This property is broadcast. What is suppressed are all the properties with respect to which the product or service is worse than its competition.

The life of a product or service is reduced by claims which are not substantiated by its use, or which are irrelevant. For example, the first ball-point pen on the market claimed that it could be used to make nine carbon copies and could even write under water. This was true, but unfortunately it could not make an original out of the water. What it did do well was leak. Like the shirts that held it, the pen had a very short life.

74. The press is the sword of Damocles that hangs over the head of every organization.

Press is a verb, not a noun. What it does is scare the hell out of executives who care more about what others think of them, particularly security analysts, than what they think of themselves.

Press coverage that is favorable is always considered to be accurate; but unfavorable coverage is always taken to be a clear distortion of the truth by a biased reporter who is ill informed, corrupt, prejudiced, and feeble minded.

To a large extent the press has come to supplement the alleged system of justice; it determines the guilt or innocence of alleged criminal or immoral acts even before they are judged in court and, in some cases, even before they are committed. It often convicts the innocent long before the alleged justice system does.

Unfortunately, it also often liberates the guilty long before the justice system does. Unlike declarations made by the criminal justice system, allegations made by the press are seldom revocable.

Even the most respected press often gives a distorted view of what is going on. The least respected press always gives a distorted view of what is not going on.

75. The more managers try to get rid of what they don't want, the less likely they are to get what they do want.

When one gets rid of what one does not want, one is likely to get something one wants even less. When DDT was used to get rid of pests it harmed things we did not want to harm. Prohibition brought a stimulus to organized crime that was much more harmful to society than abuse of alcohol.

The US has the highest percentage of its population in prison and one of the highest crime rates in the world. In our national effort to get rid of crime we intensify our efforts to catch criminals and throw them in prison. Yet studies show that, on release, a prisoner is more likely to commit a crime than before going into prison; and the resulting crime is likely to be more serious.

It is more difficult to define what we want than to point at what we do not want. Nevertheless, a "getting rid of" strategy is a cop out. Great gains are seldom made easily.

Managers should know at all times what they would have if they could have anything they wanted. The most effective way to do this is through idealized design. This involves a redesign of the organization on the assumption that it was destroyed last night. The only constraints are that the design must be technologically feasible and able to survive in the current environment. Then, the most effective way of creating the future is by reducing the gap between the current state and the state imagined by the idealized design.

76. Focusing on an organization's "core competency" diverts attention from its core competencies.

In a rapidly changing business environment, such as we have, the most important competencies are (1) the readiness, willingness, and ability to change, and (2) the ability to innovate. The absence of these competencies is more likely to result in failure than the presence of other competencies is to assure success.

However well an organization does what it currently does, it will not survive unless it learns both how to do the old things better and new things well. The ability to learn and adapt is the most important core competency an organization can have. Unfortunately, these abilities are in very short supply. Making the best horse-drawn carriage in the world did not enable its manufacturer to survive the automobile.

The average life of an American corporation has been estimated to be as low as eleven and a half years. The failures are due much more to what organizations cannot do than to what they can.

77. The greater the fee paid to corporate directors, the less their contributions are likely to be.

If directors' participation on a corporate board depends on how much they are paid, they are generally more interested in the pay than the organization. They are then often in the pocket of the CEO, operate as a rubber stamp, and expect the same in return – organizational incest.

A director should have two functions: to represent the interests of the corporation's external stakeholders, and to represent the corporation to them. In the first of these functions a director must serve as a constructive critic of corporate behavior and assure the corporation's exercise of social responsibility. Directors cannot perform this function if payment for their services depends on the extent to which they support the CEO, no matter what. A good corporate board is not the CEO's board but the CEO is the board's chief of staff. It is a board to which the CEO is beholden, not one whose members are beholden to the CEO.

78. A manager's fear of computers is directly proportional to the square of his/her age.

Pre-computer-age managers act as though personal computers bite. Children who have no such misconceptions learn how to use computers instinctively. They have the further advantage of not being able to read the instructions on their use.

Intelligent seniors learn not to use a computer without immediate access to a preschool youngster. If they try to go it alone, they are likely to get caught in a Web.

The inability to use a computer properly is as prevalent among adults as the inability to use a book properly is among youngsters. This greatly magnifies the difficulty of communication between generations.

Adults who use computers to generate conclusions tend to blame the computers for any errors that result. This is like blaming one's hand for one's illegible handwriting.

Nevertheless, most adults come to like computers because their downtimes provide more free time than holidays do.

79. Most managers know less about managing people than the conductor of an orchestra does.

Unlike a manager, the conductor of an orchestra does not tell his subordinates how to play their instruments, but how to play together. Most, if not all, members of an orchestra can play their instruments better than their conductor can. Therefore, it would be stupid as well as insulting for the conductor to instruct them on how to play their instruments. The conductor's job is not to manage their actions, but their interactions; not to supervise but to coordinate and integrate.

However, interactions can only be optimized when each individual knows how each of the others is performing. An orchestra in which none of the players could hear what the other players are doing would be cacophonous. It would not be an orchestra. In addition, they must have a common objective: one score to play.

Without a manager who focuses on interactions, who sees to it that each subordinate has the information about the others they require, and makes sure that all subordinates have a common objective, there can be no harmony.

Ackoff's F/laws: The Cake

80. Complex problems do not have simple solutions, only simple minded managers and their consultants think they do.

Panaceas in good currency prevail despite disconfirming evidence. They prevail until one alleged to be better comes along. Therefore, gullible managers ride a yo-yo manipulated by consultants and academics who produce and peddle panaceas.

The only problems that have simple solutions are simple problems. The only managers that have simple problems have simple minds. Problems that arise in organizations are almost always the product of interactions of parts, never the action of a single part. Complex problems do not have simple solutions.

Complexity is not a property of problems but of those looking at problems. Any problem that we know how to solve is simple; any that we don't is complex.

Familiarity breeds complexity. This is why the problems confronted by others, with which we have little or no familiarity, always appear to be simpler than the ones we confront ourselves.

81. When nothing can make things worse, anything can make them better.

When corporate executives are asked, "How are things?" they occasionally answer, "They couldn't be worse." What a wonderful position to be in! If this is true, then nothing can be done to make things "worser." Therefore, such a statement implies that doing anything would probably make things better. It is a time to act.

The couldn't-be-worse situation is, in one sense, much better for an organization than one about which it is said, "It couldn't be better." Nevertheless, this latter is an evaluation executives much prefer. If true, however, doing anything in such a state would make it worse. This is a worse situation than one in which doing anything can make it better. The claim that things could not be better absolves executives of the need to do anything except gloat.

There are weaker assertions that are equally effective at discouraging action: for example, "Things may not be perfect but they are good enough." "Don't rock the boat." "Let well enough alone." "Let nature take its course."

There is nothing as absolute as absolving oneself of the need to do something, anything. Such absolution eliminates any sense of guilt and, therefore, the need for confession.

82. To do more of what is not working currently, is to do more of what will not work in the future.

In most cases when a strategy or tactic is failing it is blamed on a lack of resources. When more resources are allocated to it the result is usually to make its failure more expensive. An organization arrives at maturity when it invests more in strategies and tactics that do not work than in ones that do. Witness public education in the United States.

Maturity is a state that most companies eventually reach. To break out of – or avoid – maturity, innovation is required: new products or services, new marketing or markets, more of what is different, not more of the same.

83. Those who successfully managed a company to maturity are unlikely to be able to manage it back to youth.

The best they can do is turn control over to those who have had no hand in bringing the company to its current state. Even a hysterical executive is more likely to succeed than a catatonic one.

It is not easy for an executive to admit to being an obstruction to further progress, particularly of a company whose previous growth he/she made possible. It would help if every company had a sainthood status that could be bestowed on those executives who have outlived their usefulness and hang on mercilessly.

84. Maldistribution of the work-life balance reduces morale and results in poor quality products and services.

Employees at all levels should be asked one simple question: "Assuming you were guaranteed your current salary for the rest of your life no matter what you do, what would you do tomorrow?"

If the answer is anything but, "I would come to work anyhow," their work-life balance lacks something. When this question is asked of those at the top of an organization, the answer is almost always: "I would come to work anyhow." When it is asked of those at the bottom, the answer is usually: "I would get out of here like a bat out of hell."

This leads to poor morale at lower levels in the organization and amongst those who are making the goods and delivering the services to customers.

85. Greed at the top is the fuel used to increase the maldistribution of wealth within and between corporations, and within and between societies.

The continued quest for income beyond what can be used to improve one's quality of life tends to reduce it.

One can accumulate more money than can be used to increase one's quality of life, but one can never accumulate too high a quality of life.

Ackoff's F/laws: The Cake

86. Viewing the same thing differently is not a defect: it is an advantage.

At any one time different managers will see the same thing in different ways; and the same manager will see different things in the same way at different times.

No two slices through an orange yield exactly the same view of its structure; but the more slices we examine, the more complete a picture of its structure we can formulate. It is through efforts to make different perceptions compatible that the whole truth can be approximated. The truth does not emerge from efforts to eliminate all perceptions but one. The truth is what makes it apparent that different perceptions of the same thing are, in fact, different perceptions of the same thing, not different things.

The head and tail of a coin are not views of different things, but different views of the same thing.

Different views of the same problem lead to different ways of treating it: some better than others. It is only by viewing problems differently and evaluating those differences that the most effective treatments can be found.

87. It is better to dissolve a problem than solve it.

There are four ways of treating a problem – absolution, resolution, solution, and dissolution – and the greatest of these is dissolution.

To **absolve** oneself of a problem is to ignore it and hope it will go away. This approach comes naturally to managers. It results in management by default.

To **resolve** a problem is to do what was done last time a similar thing arose OR to identify the cause of a problem and remove it, thereby returning to a previous state. It is an experience-based and common-sense approach. Problem resolution does not look for the best way of treating a problem, but settles for one that is good enough.

To **solve** a problem is to find the best that can be done in the current situation. It involves a change in the behavior of the organization that has the problem, but leaves the nature of the organization or its environment unchanged. It approaches problems quantitatively through research, including experimentation. It is exemplified by operations research and the management sciences.

To **dissolve** a problem is to redesign the organization that has the problem or its environment so the problem is eliminated and cannot reappear. An old Chinese proverb says that giving a hungry man a fish may solve his problem, but it will reoccur. Teaching him to catch fish can dissolve his problem. To cure a disease is to solve a problem. To eliminate it is to dissolve it.

88. Giving managers the information needed to (dis)solve a problem does not necessarily improve their performance.

We can only know what information is needed to (dis)solve a problem if we know how to (dis)solve it. If a way to (dis)solve a problem is known and the information required to do so is available, someone whose time is less valuable than a manager's can be given responsibility for (dis)solving it. For example, it can be given to a scientist, a staff member, a secretary or a computer.

Managers employ science but are not scientists. In other words, management is needed only where problems exists which we do not know how to (dis)solve.

89. The best way to find out how to get from here to there is to find out how to get from there to here.

This counter-intuitive principle is apparent to children who quickly learn that the best way to solve a maze is to go from the exit to the entrance. It is equally true in corporate planning.

For example, how many tennis matches must be played in a tournament in which 64 players are entered? One can find the answer by working from the beginning to the end: there would be 32 first-round matches, 16 second round, 8 third round, 4 quarter finals, 2 semi-finals, and 1 final (making 63 matches in all).

Alternatively, we can work backwards from the end of the tournament; there must be 63 losers to obtain a winner, hence 63 matches.

90. The best place to begin an intellectual journey is at its end.

And the best time to end it is when, working backwards, one reaches the beginning. The beginning is where one is now, of course.

Visionary managers always look ahead to a desired end. Whether they envision an entirely new product, a market that doesn't yet exist, or a more flexible organization structure, they know where they want to be and then work backwards to find a way of getting there.

91. Necessity may be the mother of invention, but invention is the father of desire.

People did not go around saying they wanted hand-held calculators, VCRs, digital watches, email or cell phones before they were invented. Their invention created the desire and alleged need for them.

We desire many things we do not need, and need many things we do not desire.

Needs are necessary for survival; desires are not, unless we desire what we need. We do not need most of the things we desire. We do not desire many of the things we need; we are not even conscious of needing them. Technology is driven more by desires than by needs.

92. **Managers should never accept the output of a technologically-based support system unless they understand exactly what the system does and why.**

Many managers who are unwilling to accept advice or support from subordinates whose activities they do not fully understand, are nevertheless willing to accept support from computer-based systems of whose operations they are completely ignorant.

Management information systems are usually designed by technologists who understand neither management nor the difference between data and information. Combine such ignorance with a management that does not understand the system the technologists have designed, and one has a recipe for disaster or, if lucky, large expenditures that bring no return.

93. The amount of profit that can be got from the sale of a product or service is inversely proportional to the need for it.

That's why luxury items provide the largest profit; for example, jewelry. Cheap commodities provide the least profit; for example, safety pins and potatoes.

Marketing should try to make all the things we need desirable, and to make all the other things we desire but do not need, less destructive. This has a great deal more to do with ethics than technology.

Unfortunately, technology and ethics are the twain that seldom meet.

94. Meetings that share ignorance cannot produce knowledge.

There is no amount of ignorance that, when aggregated, yields knowledge. Ten people who do not know how to do something are a much greater obstruction to learning how to do it than one. This is particularly true when they do not know that they do not know.

Managers who do not know and do not know that they do not know are fools. Ones who do not know and think they do are phonies. Managers who know but do not know that they know are so rare that we have no name for them. Moreover, they are usually unbearable.

Some managers see order when it is not there. Others do not see it when it is there. Those who see it when it is there usually have great difficulty in convincing others to this effect.

95. Employees, and even managers, are not expected to be smarter than their bosses.

It usually takes great skill to disguise the fact that they are smarter than their bosses.

However, the ability to disguise the fact is a skill that is essential for survival in most organizations.

96. Continuous improvement is the longest distance between two points: where an organization is and where it wants to be.

Continuous improvement consists of a very large number of very small improvements. These can help maintain an organization's leadership once obtained, but not for long. Continuous improvement cannot make a leader out of a company that isn't one already. However, it can make followers out of organizations that adopt it.

Only large discontinuous improvements can elevate an organization to leadership. These are creative acts, not imitative ones.

97. Benchmarking is a not-very-subtle form of imitation. It condemns organizations to following not leading.

Imitation creates followers, not leaders. Imitation of a leader cannot close the gap because organizations that lead usually have a greater ability to improve themselves than do those that imitate them.

Taking the lead requires leaping over the other: a quantum leap. It requires not taking the time to do all the things that the leader has done, but taking the time to do something the leader has not done.

98. Consensus is practical, not necessarily principled, agreement.

If consensus consisted of complete agreement between two or more decision-makers on the best possible decision, it would almost never be reached. Fortunately, consensus means agreeing that doing anything is better than doing nothing, or that doing nothing is better than doing anything. This makes it much easier to reach.

Conservatives generally believe that doing nothing is better than doing anything. Liberals generally believe that doing anything is better than doing nothing. Radicals believe that undoing everything and doing it over again is better than the other options.

Disagreements are often based on questions of fact. For example, does capital punishment decrease capital crimes? To reach consensus the agreement required is on the appropriateness of a proposed test to determine what the relevant facts are and an agreement to act as indicated by the facts.

Furthermore, it can be agreed by consensus that in an emergency the decision to act should be in the hands of a designated person. It can also be agreed that when agreement cannot be reached either that a designated person should be empowered to make the decision, or that no decision be made.

99. In a classroom, the teacher learns most.

We learn more on our own than by being taught. We learn our first language before going to school, without being taught it, but we do not learn a second language in school nearly as well. Being taught obstructs learning.

Anyone who has ever taught knows that the teacher learns the most in a classroom. Schools are upside down. Students should teach and faculty members should learn how to assist student learning. These conditions were approximated in the one-room schoolhouse, where students had to teach their juniors.

Teachers should be motivating and facilitating the self-initiated learning of others. They should be a resource for students, used as the students see fit. But students should not be used by teachers as they see fit, especially when the students are mature managers. Learning how to use others as a resource is one of the most important things anyone, especially a manager, can learn.

Most important, we learn more out of, and after, school than in it, and more by doing than by listening. Most of what a manager uses at work is learned at work, not in business school; and it is learned with the help of others who have learned it at work. No amount of academic experience makes up for a lack of relevant experience.

Ackoff's F/laws: The Cake

100. There is never a better place to initiate a change than where the one who asks where the best place is, is.

As the buck passes, it disintegrates, disappearing by the time it reaches its destination.

An organization in which no one is willing to take responsibility for initiating change is paralysed, incapable of learning and adapting to change. It is in a catatonic stupor.

101. Risk aversion is a core competency of most managers.

The pursuit of any significant change is never risk-free. But neither is the refusal to change, and this is the greater risk.

The prime principle for an individual's survival in most corporations is, "Cover thine ass."

Professionals are generally willing, as a matter of principle, to try to change, even when they face disapproval as a result. Hence they are willing to take a personal risk. Non-professionals – as many managers are – as a matter of principle are generally not willing to face disapproval or take a personal risk.

102. The more managers believe that society should be operated democratically, the less they believe that corporations should be.

Most managers in democratic societies insist that the society within which their organizations operate should operate openly and democratically. Nevertheless, they tend to manage their organizations secretively and autocratically.

Most corporations and not-for-profit organizations, including schools, hospitals and government agencies, have the same kind of political structure as did the Soviet Union. They remain hierarchical. And, even where organizations *have* become more heterarchical and their management more transparent, the behaviour of most managers or leaders under stress remains autocratic and secretive in nature.

Glasnost, as noted earlier with *Perestroika*, is as relevant to Western corporations as it was to the former Soviet Union.

103. The one thing that every individual and organization must want is the ability to obtain whatever they want.

To want anything is also to want the ability to obtain it: *competence*. Development is an increase in competence. The limit of such development is *omnicompetence*, which is the ability to get anything one might want. Omnicompetence is an ideal; it can never be attained but it can be continuously approached. Increases in competence require 4 types of progress:

◊ Science and technology: the pursuit of the *truth* and the ability to use it efficiently in the pursuit of one's ends.

◊ Economics: the pursuit of *plenty* and the resources to use the information, knowledge, and understanding that science and technology make available.

◊ Ethics and morality: the pursuit of the *good*, peace on earth and peace of mind. These require the elimination of conflict within and between individuals and groups so that their pursuit of different ends provokes cooperation not conflict.

◊ Aesthetics: the pursuit of *beauty and fun*, the stimulation and maintenance of the continuous pursuit of omnicompetence.

Like a horse-drawn wagon, development cannot move faster than its slowest horse. In our society the slowest horse is aesthetics. We have clearly made scientific and economic progress since the beginning of history, and at least some argue that we even have progressed ethically. But few if any argue that we have progressed aesthetically.

104. There is no such thing as risk-free agreement.

Progress requires the exploration and exploitation of differences, including differences between colleagues and between subordinates and their bosses.

This, of course, always involves risk. There is no such thing as a risk-free disagreement with one's colleagues or boss, which is why so few people advocate it.

What is less widely known is that there is no such thing as risk-free agreement, which is why so many people advocate it.

Groups, teams and meetings where dissent is discouraged or consensus is sought too quickly tend to end in "groupthink" – an assumed consensus around a potentially bad decision.

Executives who want clones as subordinates and subordinates who try to be clones of their bosses assure the preservation of the status quo.

Preserving the status quo and agreeing with bad decisions are both very risky ways to run a business these days.

105. CEOs should never select their successors.

When superiors select successors they tend to select ones who are not likely to perform as well as they did.

This may be done to assure retrospective admiration for that superior's superior performance (because executives like their reputations to be carried on the backs of their successors). Or it may be that the outgoing CEO cannot imagine that a very different approach could work as well as - or better than - their own (so they will not appoint someone who takes that different approach).

Either way, selecting our successors is as dangerous as selecting our children.

106. To managers, an ounce of information is worth a pound of data.

Data are symbols that represent the properties of objects and events. They are to information what iron ore is to iron: nothing can be done with data until they are processed into information.

Information also consists of symbols that represent the properties of objects and events, but these are symbols that have been processed into a potentially useful message. Information is contained in descriptions; answers to questions that begin with such words as *who*, *where*, *when*, *what*, and *how many*.

Most relevant information can be condensed significantly without loss of content. Irrelevant information can be condensed to zero without loss of content. Therefore, filtration and condensation are the two most important processes that can be applied to information. These, however, are considered to be irrelevant by those who provide managers with information. For them value and volume are synonymous.

107. To managers, an ounce of knowledge is worth a pound of information.

Knowledge is contained in instructions, answers to *how to?* questions. (Information is contained in "know that," awareness, and statements.) To know that a car won't run is information; to know how to make it work when it doesn't is knowledge.

But knowledge presupposes information just as information presupposes data. Without the information that a car needs fixing, relevant knowledge would not be applied to it. The function of knowledge is to enable one to make efficient choices from among alternatives revealed by information.

Knowledge also provides criteria for determining the relevance of information; it identifies the information required to use what is known. So information and knowledge, like Punch and Judy, presuppose each other, have no practical value when separated from each other except on quiz shows and examinations given in schools.

What an individual knows becomes organizational knowledge only when it is accessible to anybody else in the organization who has a need for it, even if the source of that knowledge is no longer part of the organization.

Knowledge is more valuable than information. Therefore, management perversely spends more time in absorbing information than in acquiring knowledge.

108. To managers, an ounce of understanding is worth a pound of knowledge.

Understanding is contained in explanations, answers to *why* questions. To know how a car works is knowledge; to know why it was designed to work the way it does is understanding.

Knowledge of how a thing works requires knowing its structure, how its parts interact. Understanding the nature of a thing requires knowing its functions in the larger systems of which it is part. For example, an automobile's function is to enable people to go from one place to another on land under their control and in privacy. It functions as part of a transportation system. The function of the accelerator is to serve the function of the car, hence the purpose of the driver.

Knowledge lets us make things work; understanding lets us make things work the way we want them to.

The defining function of a corporation is to create and distribute wealth in the societies in which it operates in and to promote the development of its stakeholders and those societies. Productive employment is the only way known to man of simultaneously producing and distributing wealth. All other ways of distributing wealth consume it.

109. To managers an ounce of wisdom is worth a pound of understanding.

This makes an ounce of wisdom worth 65,536 ounces of data, using the previous three f/laws:

1oz wisdom = 1lb understanding

1oz understanding = 1lb knowledge

1oz knowledge = 1lb information

1oz information = 1lb data

Wisdom is contained in value statements, e.g. aphorisms and proverbs. It lets us perceive and evaluate the long-term as well as short-term consequences of what we do. It induces us to want to pursue things of lasting value. It enables us to make short-run sacrifices for long-run gains. It prevents our sacrificing the future for the present.

Knowledge enables us to make things work; understanding enables us to make things work the way we want; wisdom enables us to want the "right" things, things that increase our ability to obtain what we and others need and want.

Information, knowledge, and understanding enable us to do things right, to be efficient, but wisdom enables us to do the right things, to be effective. Science pursues data, information, knowledge, and understanding: what is truth; but the humanities pursue wisdom: what is right.

110. Giving managers the information they want may not improve their performance.

The genius of managers, where it exists, lies in their ability to manage efficiently systems they do not completely know or understand. Where knowledge and understanding are lacking, there is no criterion for determining what constitutes relevant information. Without such criteria it is intuition that plays the key role. The quality of their intuitions differentiates managers more than the quality of what they know and understand.

When managers who lack relevant knowledge and understanding are asked what information they want, they play it safe by saying, "Everything." The result is an increase in the manager's information overload and in the time that must be spent filtering out what is relevant.

The genius of science lies in its ability to manage efficiently systems that are understood. But science is incapable of managing efficiently any system that is not understood. So, science gives management the platform from which, using intuition, it can jump into uncertainty. But it should be borne in mind that managers jump, not scientists, and so the risks and responsibilities associated with decision-making are not shared equally. In fact, they are not shared at all.

111. Rightsizing consists of wronging a right.

Rightsizing is a euphemism for downsizing. It is actually wrongsizing, because those who are laid off are seldom responsible for the condition that their layoffs are supposed to correct. Those who fire them are usually responsible for that condition.

To rightsize is to reduce over-employment, which is a symptom, not a disease. The disease consists of the presence of internal units that are monopolistic providers of essential services to other internal units that do not pay for these services directly.

Internal service monopolies are subsidized by an amount proportional to their size. So they try to grow continually by creating "make work." Because users have no choice of supplier, the suppliers are not responsive to their users' needs and desires.

Furthermore, they have little incentive to serve them efficiently. Downsizing may reduce the size of internal service units but it does not change their *modus operandi* – which involves generating make-work and adding excess personnel. When competition forces corporations to cut costs, they frequently resort to downsizing because their internal monopolies continually resort to upsizing. Downsizing is endemic to organizations whose internal service providers are bureaucratic monopolies. An internal market economy is the only effective way of eliminating bureaucratic monopolies within the firm.

112. Improving communication between the parts of an organization may destroy it.

The more information hostile parties have about one another, the more harm each can inflict on the other. If, in wartime, neither party had any information about the other they would be unable to inflict any harm or destruction on the other. Of course, it is equally true that the more information friendly parties have about each other the more help they can give each other. Therefore, communication has value only among cooperating parties.

However, as Peter Drucker once observed, there is more conflict within corporations than between them, and it is generally less ethical. Therefore, unless such conflict is eliminated, improved communication within a firm can hurt it, even destroy it.

Effective alignment of objectives is essential if communication is to benefit communicating parties. Such alignment can only occur when performance of the whole organization is the primary criterion employed in evaluating performance of any of the parts.

113. The stability of a family business and of the family that owns it are inversely proportional to the number of family members employed in the business.

Sons seldom believe that father knows best or, as a matter of fact, that anyone other than themselves does. A family business brings out the worst in relatives, particularly in those whose best is not very good. The competition for power in the business among siblings tends to carry over into the family and is as destructive to the family as it is to the business.

Members of a family know each other's weaknesses better than the weaknesses of any outsider. Therefore, they tend to trust each other less than outsiders, and with good reason.

Competence is not an inherited characteristic. It tends to diminish with successive generations. A competent offspring is a mutant, not a product of systemic evolution.

114. Communication is never good in itself.

This is a common misapprehension.

Communication is only a means to ends that may be bad as well as good. It should be kept in mind that although some communication may be good, there is an amount of it, as for anything, that is bad.

Witness spam!

115. The prominence of a business author is proportional to the number of times he or she has published the same article or book.

Nothing breeds more business books than a successful business book. Follow-ups are like sequels to a successful movie. They continue as long as the author/producer is alive and those who read/saw the first book/movie no longer remember it.

A change in punctuation or format is sufficient reason for a new edition of a successful book no matter how bad it is. But no type of change is sufficient reason for republishing an unsuccessful book, no matter how good it is.

This last statement is not quite true: if more sex could be introduced into unsuccessful books they just might sell – especially if illustrated. But it is as hard to make books on management sexy as it is to make managers sexy.

Finally, no author has ever read all the books he or she cites.

116. **Organizations fail more often because of what they have not done than because of what they have done.**

Similarly, it is worse to deny a truth than accept a falsehood. But errors of omission are seldom recorded and accounted for. So, executives who cannot get away unpunished for doing something they should not have done, can usually get away with not doing something they should have done.

Since errors of commission are the only type of mistake accounted for, a security-seeking manager's optimal strategy is to avoid such errors by doing as little as possible, including nothing. The most successful executives are those who can create the appearance of doing a great deal without doing anything. Herein lies the root of an organization's disinclination to change.

117. The quality of a business school is inversely proportional to the amount of teaching its faculty does and is directly proportional to the amount of on-the-job learning in which the faculty and students engage.

The higher the ranking of a business school, the lower is the average teaching load of its faculty members and the less time they spend at the institution. The moral is clear: business schools would attain the highest possible rank if no teaching was done and faculty members were never present.

It is ironic that schools that try to minimize the amount of teaching their faculty must do, also try to maximize the amount of teaching to which their students are subjected. This maximizes the number of faculty members required per square student.

Business schools give students the illusion of relevant learning: an illusion later dispelled at work. Business school students learn a vocabulary that enables them to speak authoritatively on subjects they do not understand. They also learn a set of principles that have demonstrated their ability to withstand large amounts of disconfirming evidence.

Finally, business schools provide a ticket of admission to a job on which relevant learning can begin.

Ackoff's F/laws: The Cake

118. Successful management consultants are ones who support managers' unsupportable beliefs.

Managers' strongest opinions are ones for which there is no supporting evidence. This follows from the fact that the reputations of managers depend to a large extent on their ability to convey the impression of infallibility to their peers and superiors. (Their subordinates *always* know how fallible they are.)

Managers' infallibility-complexes are reflected in the fact that they never express doubt or consult a reference or authority when confronted with a problem while in the presence of others.

All this explains why managers prefer consultants who produce the appearance of proof for what those same managers accept without proof.

119. Problems are not objects of experience, but mental constructs extracted from it by analysis.

Problems are abstractions. What managers actually experience are messes, which are complex systems of interacting problems. Problems are to messes what atoms are to desks. We experience desks, not the atoms they are made of; we experience messes, not the problems they are made of.

No problem can be solved without affecting others in the system of which it is a part, usually without exacerbating them. A solution to a problem taken separately can create a much more serious problem than the problem thereby solved.

One can get rid of a bad heart by having it removed. One can avoid food poisoning by not eating. Solving problems taken separately can be a very dangerous thing.

120. It is better to control the future imperfectly than to forecast it perfectly.

For example, we would rather work in a building within which the weather is controlled, than out of doors even if we had a perfect forecast of the weather and access to all the clothing we would want.

Control of oneself and one's immediate environment eliminates the need to forecast or control the less immediate environment. And, indeed, the rapidity of change makes reliable forecasting harder than ever to do well.

So the objective of planning should not be to prepare for a future that is out of our control, but to control that future in the way that buildings control future weather.

121. Competition is conflict embedded in cooperation.

Two tennis players in a friendly match are in conflict with respect to winning. But they cooperate over a more important shared objective: recreation and exercise. The more intense their conflict, the more fun and exercise they derive from the match. If the cooperative objectives, fun and exercise, do not dominate the conflicting objective, winning, then the match becomes a fight.

Competition is conflict according to rules designed to ensure cooperation. When the rules are broken, cooperation evaporates and conflict alone remains. This is why competition needs a referee to ensure the rules are followed.

In economic competition conflict between alternative suppliers of goods and services is intended to serve the interests of consumers. If competitors collude to bilk consumers, as in price fixing, they stop competing, cooperate with each other and conflict with consumers. Government is supposed to be the referee that makes the rules to prevent economic competition turning into conflict or pure cooperation. But government is a supplier of regulations that are for sale in the lobby.

Ackoff's F/laws: The Cake

122. How far an organization can evade government regulations is proportional to the amount it contributed to the election of successful candidates.

Lobbyists are lawyers who no longer practice law; they buy it. Elected officials whose campaigns are financed by corporations sell the law to them. Together they form a vicious circle from which the public cannot escape. The circumference of the circle is directly proportional to the number of organizations the officials are willing to "accommodate." *Accommodate* is a euphemism.

Executives who engage in evasions of the law sometimes "get caught." This usually involves a length of time between their exposure and trial that exceeds their time to retirement or death.

Those executives who serve a term in prison wear it like a badge of honor when they come out. They are taken to be martyrs to the corporate cause.

The Leader & His Followers.

The Authors

Ackoff

At the time of his death, Russell L. Ackoff was the Anheuser-Busch Emeritus Professor of Management Science at The Wharton School, University of Pennsylvania. He wrote numerous books on Systems and Design Thinking, including *Idealized Design* (with Jason Magidson and Herbert J. Addison), Re-Designing the Corporation, and Ackoff's Best. His last two books were *Memories* and *Differences that make a Difference*.

A founding member of the Institute of Management Sciences, his work in consulting and education involved more than 350 corporations and 75 government agencies in the United States and beyond. Management grandee, he was often ranked high in lists of the world's most influential business thinkers. But he refused to allow people to call him a guru.

Addison

Herbert J. Addison has worked for some 40 years in academic, educational and business book publishing, including for many years at Oxford University Press. He is the author of the business section in the *New York Times Guide to Essential Knowledge* and was a close friend of Russ Ackoff.

Ackoff's F/laws are available in print as follows:

Nos. 1-81 (with a considered response to each f/law by Sally Bibb and with Ackoff's own illustrations) are published by Triarchy Press as *Management f-Laws: How Organizations Really Work*.

Nos. 82-122 (with an extended introduction to Systems Thinking and with more of Ackoff's own illustrations) are published by Triarchy Press as *Systems Thinking for Curious Managers*.

Tenure

About Triarchy Press

Triarchy Press is a small, independent publisher of good books in the field of organizational and social praxis.

Praxis is the cyclical process by which we apply theories and skills in practice, reflect on our experience, refine those theories and skills, and then apply them again in practice.

We look for the best new thinking on the organizations and social structures we work and live in. And we explore the most promising new practices in these areas. We try, in particular, to bridge academic research/theory and practical experience.

Our books cover innovative approaches to designing and steering organizations, the public sector, teams, society, and the creative life of individuals.

To submit your own f/law or find out about ordering multiple copies of this book, which can be printed with your logo or other personalization, please visit www.f-laws.com.

Other Systems Thinking titles from Triarchy Press

Growing Wings on the Way: Systems Thinking for Messy Situations is a guide for applying Systems Thinking in practice.

Systems Thinking in the Public Sector is John Seddon's famous critique of public sector management.

Memories is Russ Ackoff's delightful account of his work with the US Army, the Queen of Iran and many other unexpected clients.

Differences that make a Difference is Ackoff's glossary of linguistic misunderstandings. 'A manual for clear thinking...' Charles Handy.

For the full list of Systems Thinking titles please visit
www.triarchypress.com/systemsthinking

www.triarchypress.com

tp